I Can't Remember
If I'm the
Good Sister
or the
Evil One

ISBN-13: 978-0-7407-7706-6

ISBN-10: 0-7407-7706-8

Library of Congress Control Number: 2008921597

08 09 10 11 12 TWP 10 9 8 7 6 5 4 3 2 1

Licensed by Creatif

www.coedikit.com

www.andrewsmcmeel.com

ATTENTION: SCHOOLS AND BUSINESSES
Andrews McMeel books are available at quantity discounts with bulk purchase for
educational, business, or sales promotional use. For information, please write to: Special
Sales Department, Andrews McMeel Publishing, LLC, 1130 Walnut Street, Kansas City,
Missouri 64106.

I Can't Remember If I'm the Good Sister or the Evil One

Cheryl Caldwell

a Co-edikit® book

**Andrews McMeel
Publishing,LLC**

Kansas City

When we were growing up,
we sometimes argued about the silliest things.

The LAST thing I want to do
is annoy you.

But it's definitely on the list!

remember
if I'm the
GOOD
sister
or the
EVIL
one!

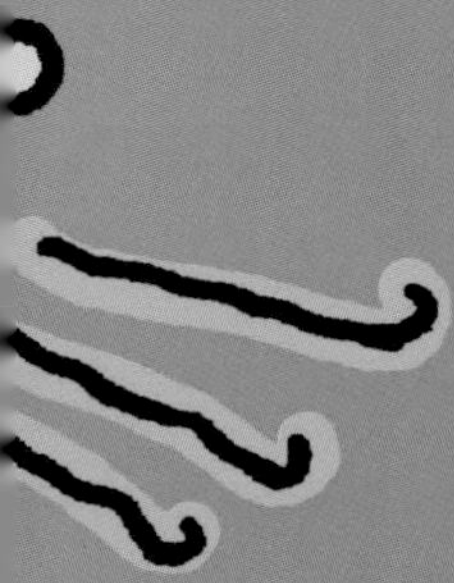

In truth you could probably have said both of us.

when
boys
think,

As we've grown and
matured,

their
brains
explode.

you've become someone
to lean on,

to count on,

and every now and then still someone
   to tell on!

Gobble!

Gobble!

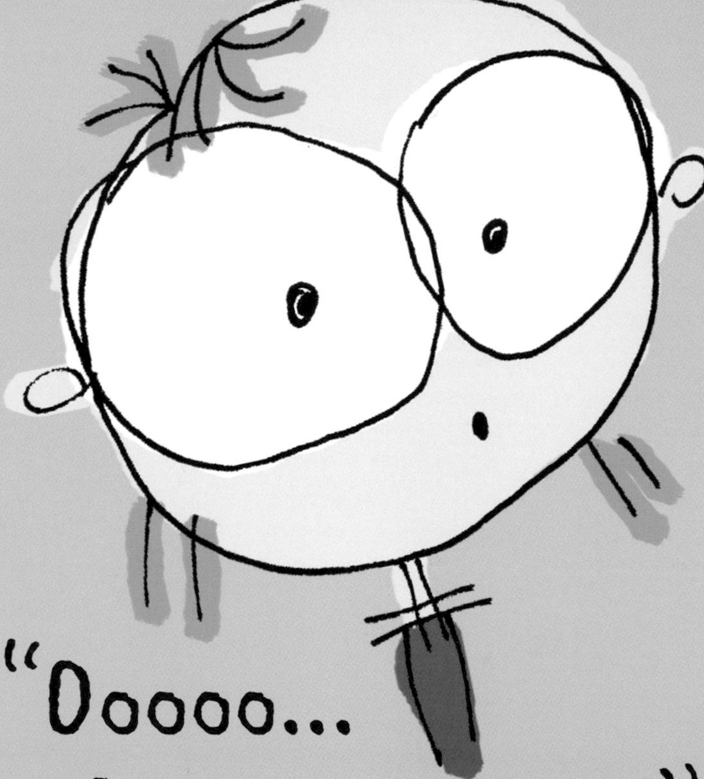

"Ooooo...
such fowl language!"

You've loved me when
I've been full of joy,

I'm sorry but I'm all out of nice.

full of myself,

2Cute4U

or full of crap.

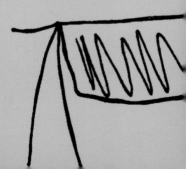

bull stick

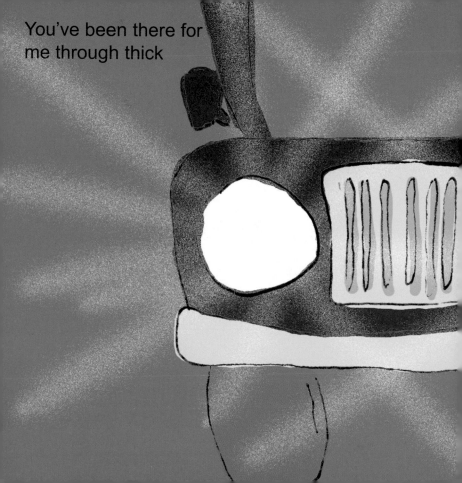

You've been there for
me through thick

Everything's
going my way
(uh-oh, I'm in the wrong lane).

and thin.

And so, I've always known I could count on you to be there for me

we're all here

because

we're not

all there!

and with me.

where are we going
and
why are we in this handbasket?

You put up with my moods.

PMS:
When Good Girls Go Bad.

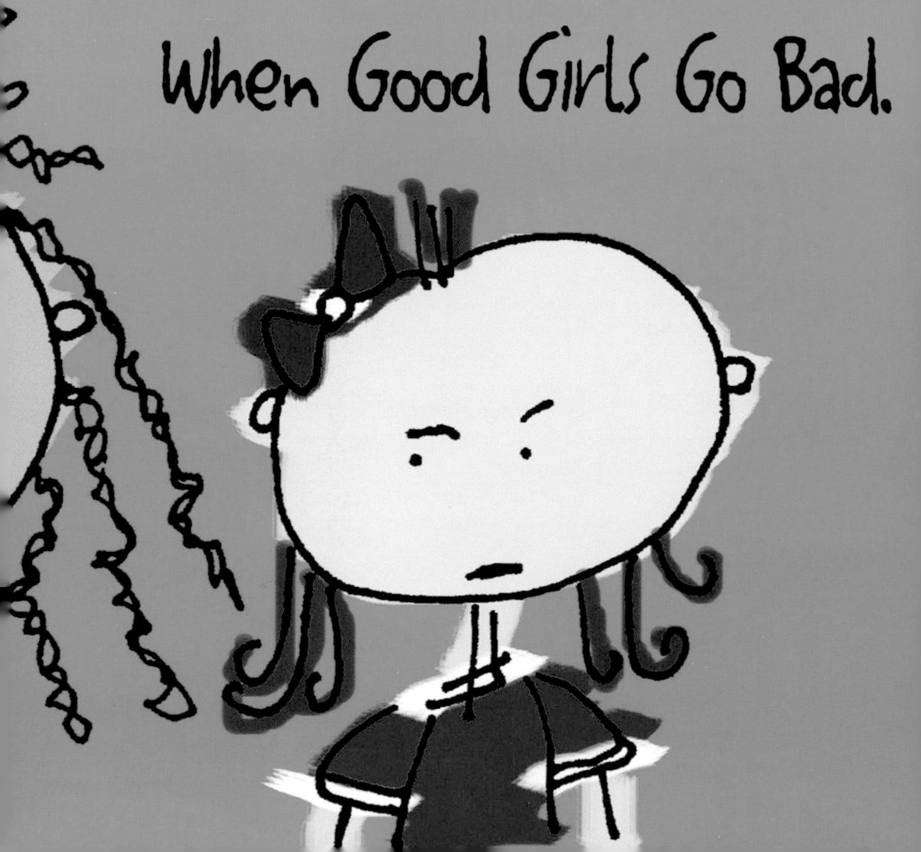

And deal with my idiosyncrasies.

You can call me
Pork Chop.

Don't make me

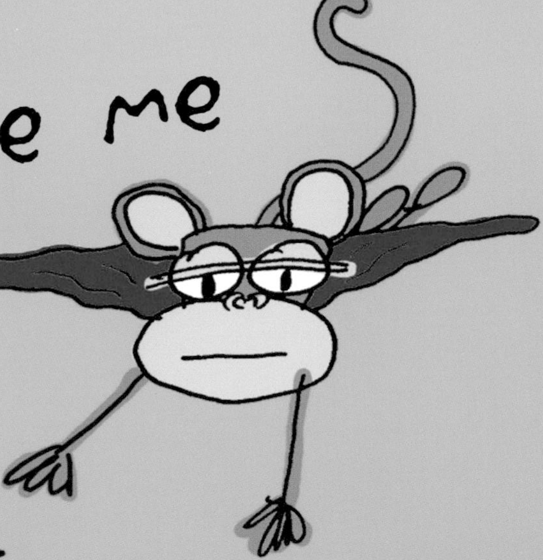

get my flying monkeys!

and my constant ally.

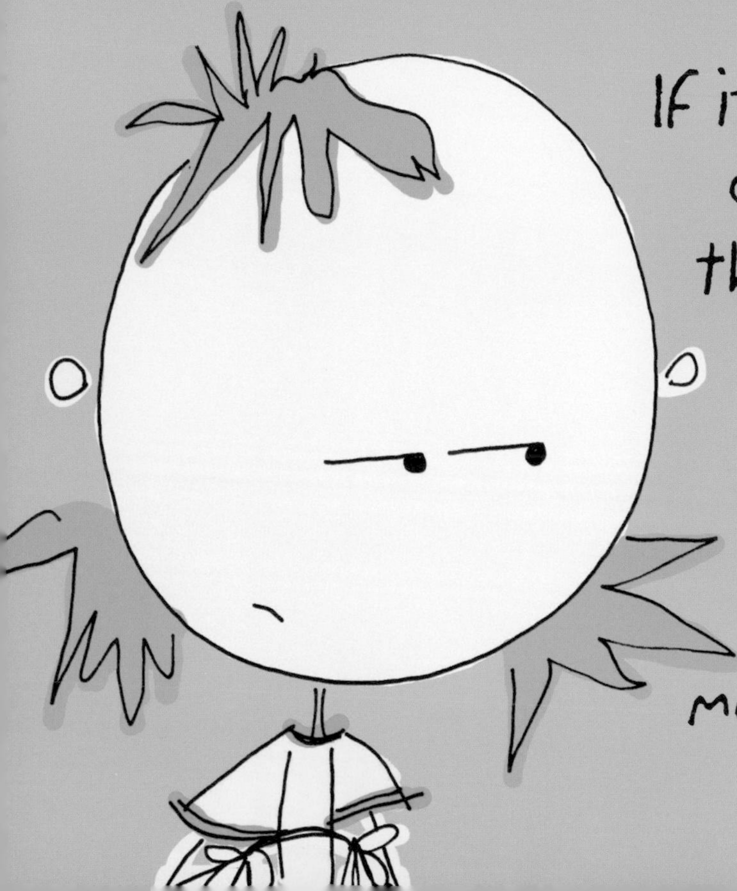

If it's not one thing...

it's our mother.

You've been my sounding board,

Take my advice.

I
don't
use it
anyway.

my confidant,

Enough about
You,

what about
me!?!

my co-conspirator,

Is it time for
your medication
or mine?

and my best friend.

When I'm
lucky enough
to be
with you,

With you, I have the freedom to
share my innermost thoughts,

The little men
who live in my head and
scream into my ear
said to tell you "Hi!"

to pursue my dreams,

Follow your dreams

(except for that one where you go to work naked and dance the polka).

and to simply be myself.

You call me
a BEACH,
like it's a
BAD thing!

and downs.

I've fallen...

and I can't

We've seen each other
through love

Love
me
or
leave
me.

and loss.

My psychic boyfriend
left me before we met.

I heard it through the
apevine.

about really important
things

or absolutely nothing at all.

Shoes are life.

The rest are just accessories.

You've helped me develop new talents

Drama Queen

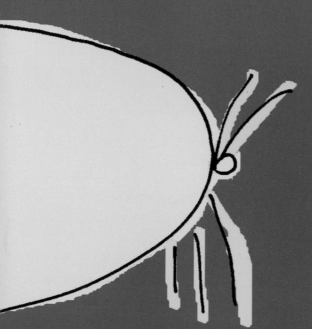

but my aim
is getting better.

You praise my accomplishments

I is a college graduate.

and honor my convictions.

they just
look older.

(What were your other 2 wishes?)

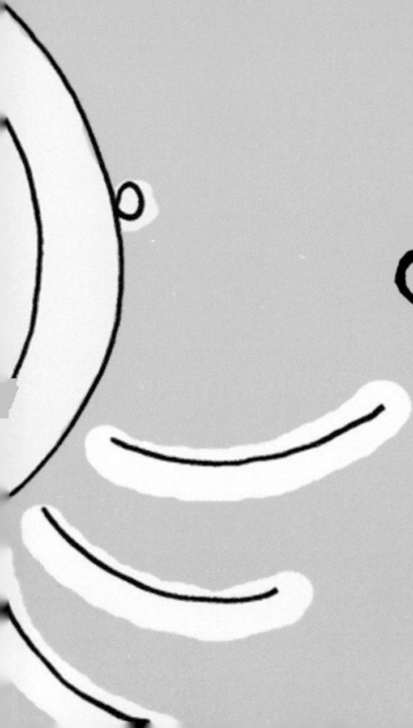

surely
someone will find
you and bring you back!

you are always right here in my heart.